The Ribber

Donna Peters

The Ribber

Table of Contents

Introduction

Thank you for purchasing this second Sock Knitting Machine book, I will continue this book where book one left off. If you do not have book one you can order a copy on www.CountryRain.com

- For this book you will need to have your sock machine in working order.
- You will also need Sock Yarn (Regia or Opal brands work good)
  and new ribber needles.

And as I said in Book One, these procedures are the ways I do things on the sock machine, these things work for me, you may need to modify some of the things I show you to make it work for you.

My best advice to you is to attend crank-in's, the annual CSMSA Conference, or just get together with other CSM owners and see how others do things, share your ideas.

The ribber will enable your sock machine to make purl stitches. Ribbing can be done for the leg of the socks, and you can also rib down the top of the foot.

This book is not a pattern book; it is a step by step approach to show you how to use your ribber.

RIBBER PARTS

Ribber Arm

The ribber arm supports the ribber dial and tappet plate. When in use you set the ribber into the holes on the side of the Cam Shell.

Ribber Dial

This is a flat disk with slots around it for the ribber needles. When the ribber is used you will be creating the purling stitches.

Make sure you use the correct ribbed dial for the cylinder you have in your machine. A ribber dial will normally have half the number of slots as the cylinder.

Auto Knitter Tappet Plate

The tappet plate rests on top of the ribber dial. The tappet plate contains cams also and these cams tell the ribber needles what path to follow to create the rib or purl stitches.

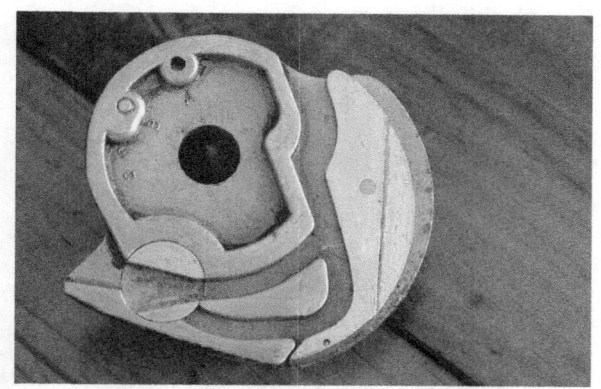

This is the underside of an Auto Knitter tappet plate.

The Ribber

Gearhart ribbers

Gearhart tappet plate

The Ribber

Legare Sock Machine Ribber

Master Sock Machine Ribber

Cylinder Ribber Guide

You may only have this guide if you have a ribber. This guide is used to adjust the needle placement on the ribber.

Also note that a Gearhart machine will have this ribber guide mounted in the cylinders permanently.

Ribber Drive Pin

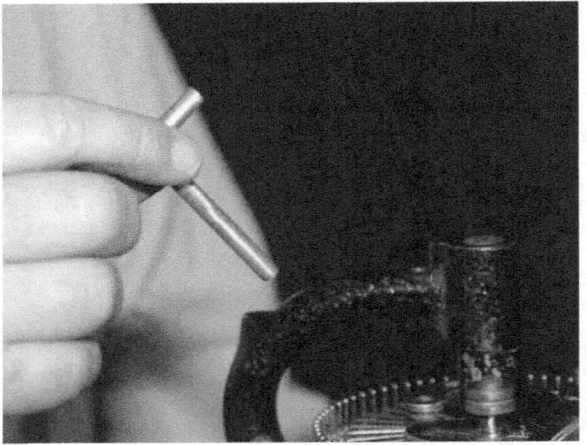

The drive pin is found on Legare, Auto Knitter, and Master machines to name a few. Gearhart machines do not have drive pin.

HOW TO INSTALL THE CYLINDER RIBBER GUIDE

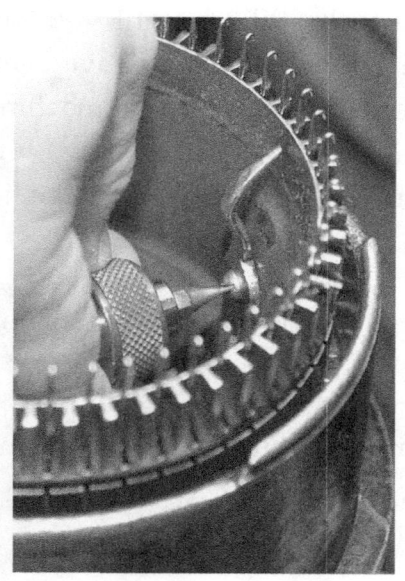

For a Auto Knitter or a Legare machine place the cylinder ribber guide in the cylinder it will screw into the cylinder hole on the left with a small screw. The bottom of the ribber guide rests in the groove of the ribber dial adjustment screw. It helps to have a short handle screwdriver to get this screw in.

Gearhart machines do not have one of these guides, the cylinders for all Gearhart machines have these posts made as part of the cylinder.

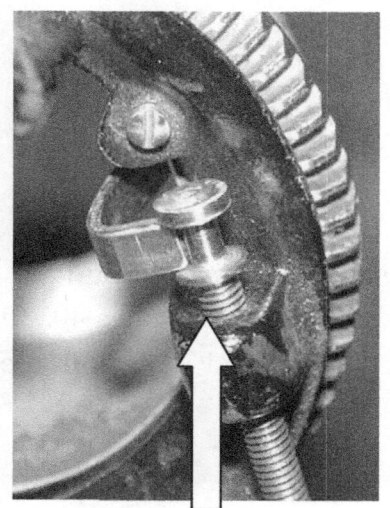

View from below so you can see how this rests in the dial adjustment.

It does not wrap around the post, it rests gently in the slot.

How to Use the Ribber

In many of the old sock machine manuals they say Not to try the Ribber until you can successfully knit socks. I recommend that you do not try the ribber until you have been able to knit without getting holes in your socks. The ribber goes on the top of the machine and will cover up the cylinder hole, so you are not able to see inside like you can now. It is kind of like putting the lid on the pot when you are cooking and not being able to lift the lid up to check out what you are cooking.

The ribber is not hard to use, it is different in that you cannot see inside the cylinder as you could which does take a little getting used to.

Before you start to use the ribber make sure your sock machine is knitting tubes with no dropped stitches.

BABY STEPS

What we are going to do is start to use the ribber first with no yarn so you can see how the ribber works first, and then we will add only one needle. With this one needle we will ensure it is all working correctly. After you have one needle working correctly, then we will start knitting tubes with the ribber in place.

Use the correct ribber dial

The ribber will have half the number of slots as your cylinder, so for example if you have a 60 slot cylinder your ribber dial would be 30 slots, an 80 slot cylinder would have a 40. On a Legare machine you will normally have a 36 slot ribber that can be used with both a 54 and a 72 slot cylinder.

HOW DOES THE RIBBER WORK?

Do these steps to learn how it all works first with NO KNITTING OR YARN on the machine, when you do not have any yarn on the machine ALWAYS crank SLOW so you do not bend any of the latches on the needles.

First look at your Cylinder on the machine, you will see a silver pointer near the left side of the cylinder this is the Cylinder Ribber Guide.

If you do not have this guide installed you will need to install it.

Gearhart machines have this guide on the cylinders permanently. It should be at the rear of your machine. If your Gearhart cylinder does not have the guide you will not be able to use the ribber with that cylinder.

Next locate the large round screw that is also on the left side of the machine, the Ribber Dial Adjustment sits on it.

This screw is what is used to adjust the location of the ribber slots to the slots on the cylinder

Do not adjust this screw yet.

The Ribber

Lets look at the Ribber

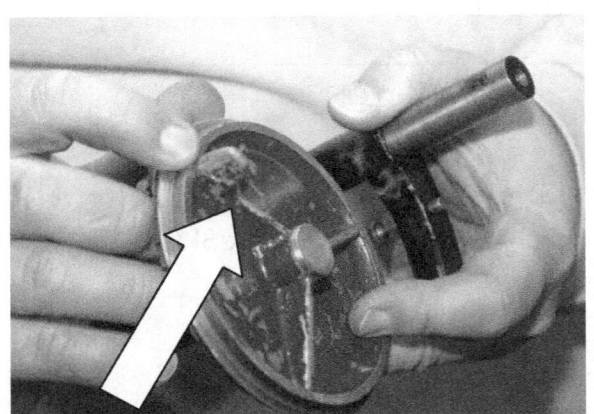

On the bottom of the Ribber Dial is the tongue or fin this fin will butt up against the Ribber Dial Guide on the machine when you put the ribber on the machine.

Put the ribber on the machine, with No Needles in the Ribber, use your fingers to turn the Ribber Dial (the one with slots) Counter Clockwise till it stops or butts up against the Ribber Dial Guide in the machine.

The Ribber

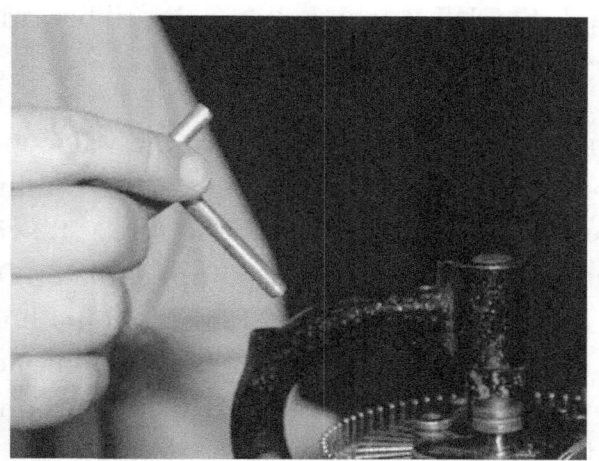

If your ribber drive pin is not installed place it in the hole on the ribber arm. Make sure it goes in all the way and is touching the tappet plate.

If you have a Gearhart machine they do not have a ribber drive pin.

For a Auto Knitter the drive pin will go in the hole on the tappet plate

Crank <u>SLOWLY</u> you will see the ribber arm move with the machine.

On a Legare machine the Drive Pin will come around and butt up against the timing screw when this pin meets the screw it will then start turning the Ribber Tappet plate. On an Auto Knitter the Drive Pin sits in the hole on the tappet plate. The ribber dial will not move, the tappet plate is what will go around and around.

One Needle

Put One needle in the ribber so you can see how the ribber needles work

and STILL WITH NO YARN in the machine

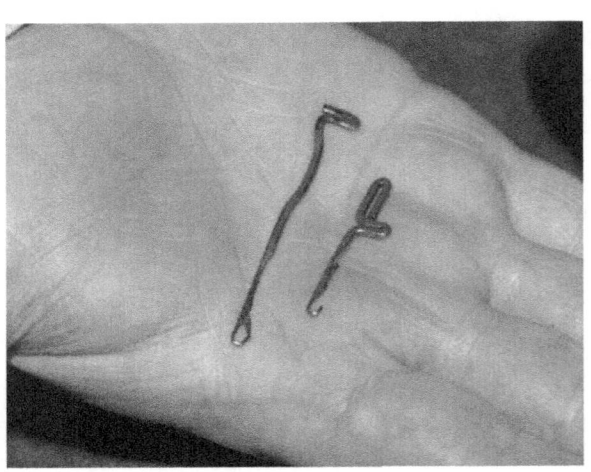

The ribber needles are shorter than the cylinder needles.

Looking at the ribber dial the one with the slots, find one slot that is even with a needle on the cylinder, it does not matter which one but make it one in the front of the machine so you can see the needle movement. You may need to move the ribber dial so it is hitting the Ribber Guide snuggly by placing your finger on the dial.

Now take that one Cylinder needle out pull the needle up, and then out from the spring

Take one of your ribber needles and slide it in the slot on the ribber dial

Make sure the ribber needle is in the center of the slot on the cylinder.

If you need to align the ribber so that the ribber needle is in the center of the cylinder slot.

To move the dial forward - turn the large round screw to the right

To move the dial backward- turn the large round screw to the left

As you are adjusting this keep your fingers on the ribber dial and keep pressing the dial so the fin on the underside of the ribber is keeping in contact with the ribber adjuster

Start turning the crank very slowly

look at that ribber needle you put in the slot and make sure it is still centered in the slot,

PLEASE NOTE: When you do not have yarn on the needles the latches will not open or shut. The needles need yarn on them to work.

Keep cranking slowly and as the butt of the ribber needle goes into the ribber tappet the needle will come out this is what will grasp the yarn as it is coming around.

Crank around a couple more times just to get the feel for what the ribber is doing.

Cranking slowly so you do not bend any of the needle latches.

USING THE RIBBER WITH YARN

Let's try the ribber with yarn this time, and again we will only be using <u>one ribber needle</u>. By using only one ribber needle you are able to see what the sock machine is doing, and if you run into trouble you will only have a mess on one needle which is much better then on 20+ needles. ☺

In the directions that follow is how things should work, if you are having trouble getting your machine to rib with the one needle Please see the section in this book for Items To Check If You Are Having Trouble.

To start using the ribber use Sock yarn, after you get the hang of it you can use different weight yarns but it is easier to learn the ribber with Sock weight yarn.

Start your machine knitting with all the cylinder needles producing a tube, knit a tube least 8 inches long, tie on your sock yarn

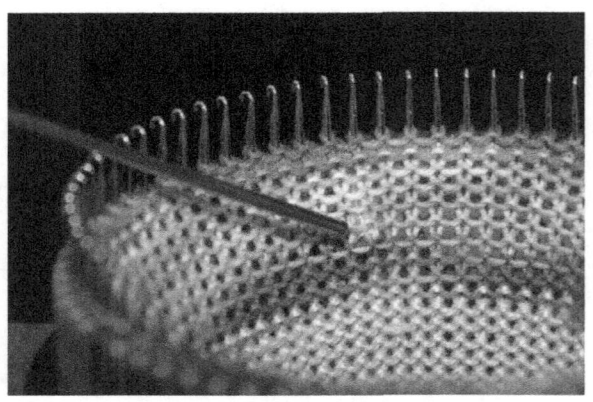

Locate the cylinder ribber guide on your cylinder; this is where the ribber fin is going to stop.

It may be harder to find when there is knitting on the machine but you will be able to feel it.

Place your ribber on your machine

When you set the ribber arm down into the holes on the cam shell ensure you are getting the ribber seated all the way down into the holes on the cam shell.

Use your fingers to move the ribber dial counter clockwise till the tongue or fin butts up against the cylinder ribber guide.

Make sure the ribber tongue is really hitting the adjustment and not just hung up on your knitted tube.

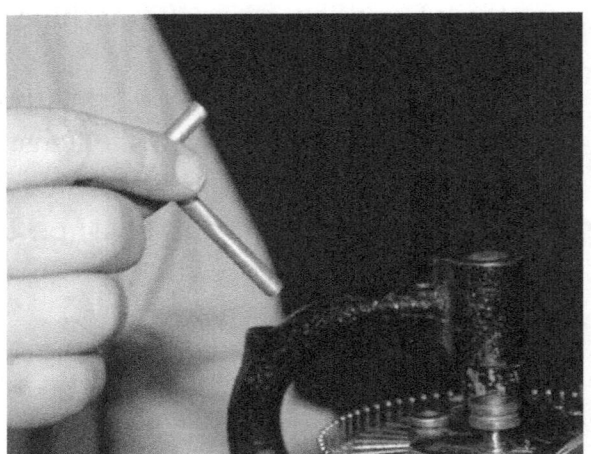

Insure your ribber drive pin is installed in the ribber arm.

If you have an Auto Knitter the drive pin will go in the hole pictured.

If you have a Gearhart machine they do not have a ribber drive pin

Look at the ribber slots and find One (only do one to start) slot that is centered above one slot on the cylinder.

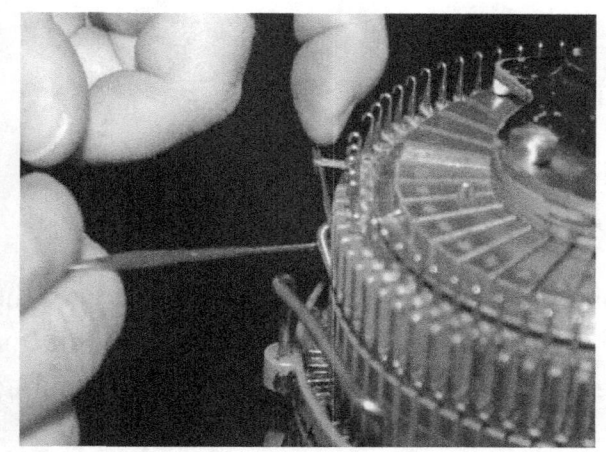

Locate your spring holder on the cam shell and crank around so the spring holder is in front of the needle you are going to remove.

By pulling a needle out a little this will release the spring that is holding the needles in the cylinder out. Take your crochet hook and pull the spring and place it on the spring holder.

Some machines may not have a spring holder.

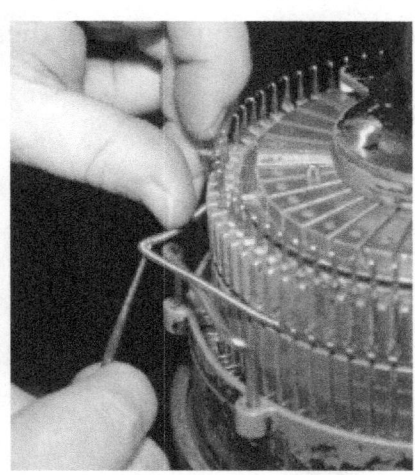

We are now going to transfer one cylinder stitch to a ribber needle.

The main goal here is to get the stitch that is on the cylinder needle transferred to the ribber needle without dropping it.

I have seen MANY ways to do this, how it is done does not matter. Your goal is to get the stitch transferred in what ever method works for you.   I will show you how I do it, but this is one place where you will have to find the method you feel the most comfortable using. Experiment and find a way you like.

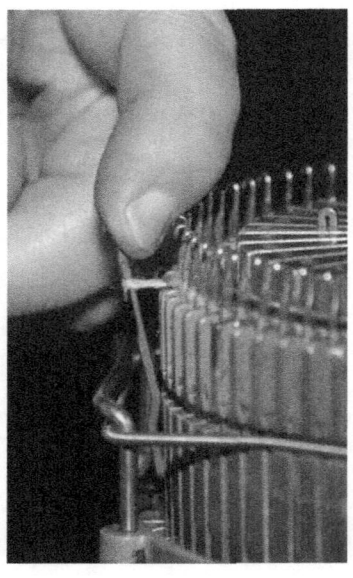

I Push the cylinder needle out a little to get a gap or so you can see the loop of the stitch.

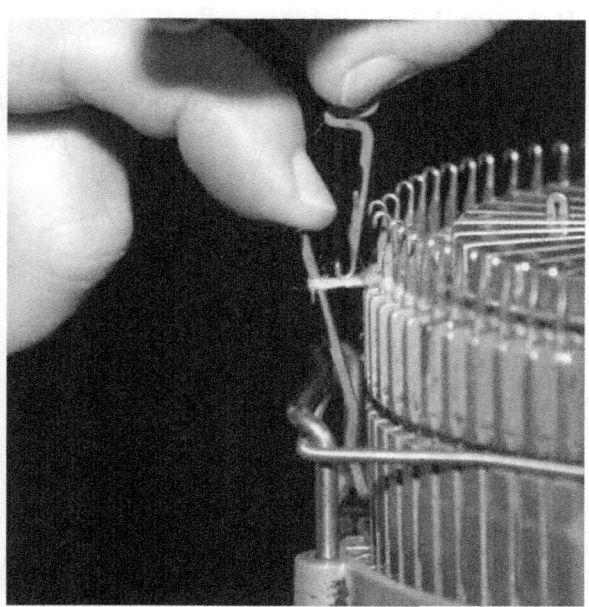

Put the hook of the ribber needle into the loop on the cylinder needle

Place the ribber needle butt into the slot

During this step the stitch is still on the cylinder needle also

Ensure the stitch is on the ribber needle

Remove the cylinder needle

And push the butt of the ribber needle back into the slot.

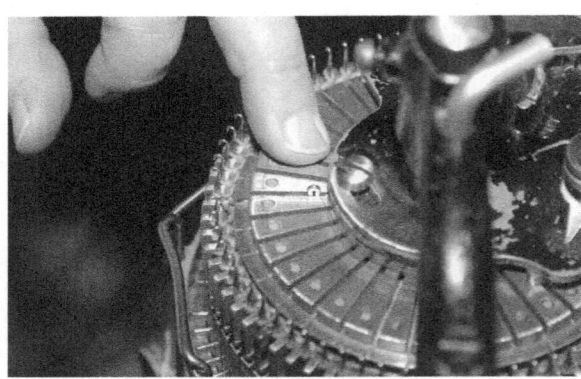

Ensure the butt of the ribber needle is all the way in.

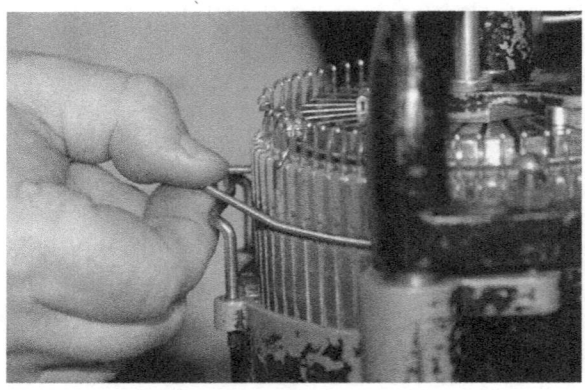

After you have the ribber needle in and the cylinder needle out, place the cylinder spring back on the cylinder to hold the needles.

And crank around slowly and ensure the ribber needle catches the yarn as it travels past it.

If your ribber needle is not knitting, please see the section in this book called

Items to Check If You Are Having Trouble.

As the ribber works you will see the ribber needles extending out. As the yarn coming from the yarn carrier lays on top of the ribber needle the needle will then start to get pulled back into the tappet

After this one needle is knitting correctly, find the next ribber slot that matches the cylinder slot.

The photo was taken on a Auto Knitter, showing a 1x1 rib

On a Legare with a 54 slot cylinder and 36 slot ribber it will be every other ribber slot that will match or a 2x1 rib

Start putting more ribber needles in around the dial.

HOW TO SWITCH RIBBER NEEDLES BACK TO CYLINDER NEEDLES

Now that you have your machine ribbing, you are going to want to switch the needles back so you have all the cylinder needles in.

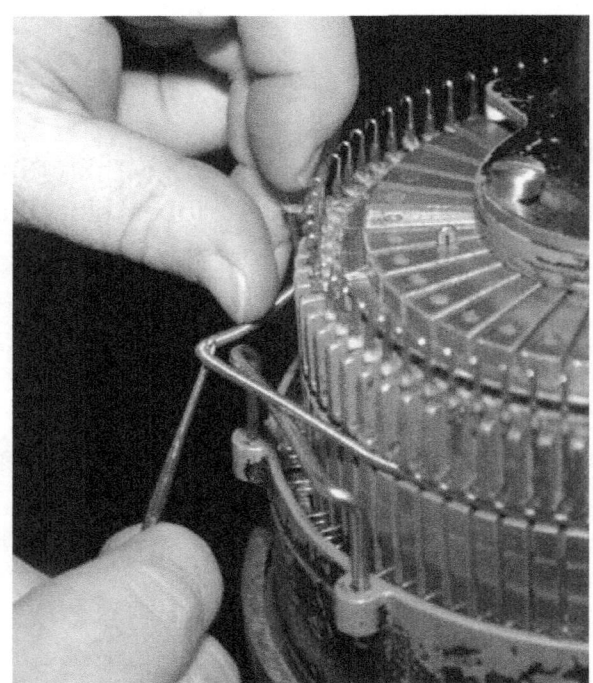

Place your cylinder spring on the spring holder.

Again your Goal is to get the stitch that is now on your Ribber needle transferred to the cylinder needle. And as I said before you need to find the method of doing this that works for you. It does not matter how you do this.

As long as you get the stitch transferred and do not drop it you did it correct.

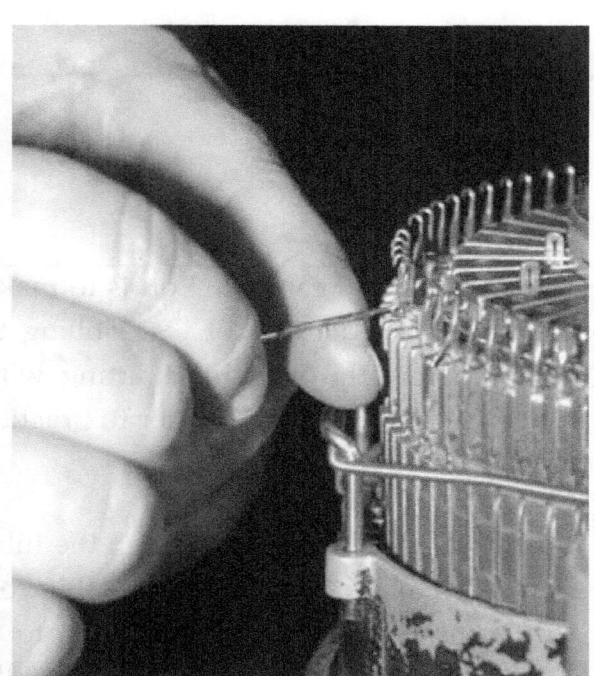

Use the cylinder needle to gently pull the ribber needle out. You will feel it pop as the stitch comes off over the latch.

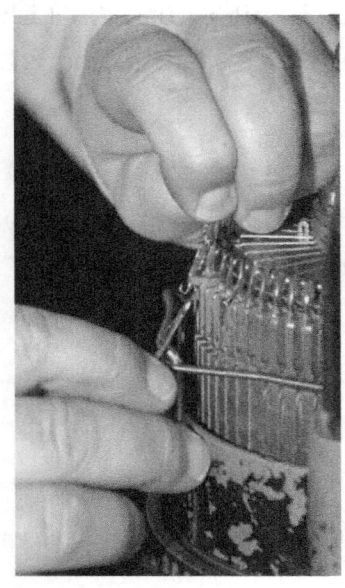

Grab onto the ribber needle and pull it out so you can see the loop of the stitch.

Now take the cylinder needle and place the hook end into the loop.

When the cylinder needle has the stitch on it, place the cylinder needle into the slot on the cylinder. And remove the ribber needle.

KNITTING RIBBED TUBES

The best advice I can give you is to make a couple knitted tubes of just ribbing to get a feel for the machine knitting with the ribber on. It is much better to practice with a tube and not a real sock.

Change maybe half way through the tube from a 1x1 rib to a 3x1 rib. To do this you will transfer 2 ribber needles out to 2 cylinder needles. Leave one ribber needle then transfer 2 more ribber to cylinder all the way around the machine.

Knitting with the ribber on will produce a knit / purl fabric. Depending on your machine, cylinder / ribber combinations you can produce a 1x1 rib (1 knit 1 purl) 2x1 (2 knit 1 purl) 3x1 (3 knit 1 purl) etc. A 1x1 rib will produce a tighter fabric then say a 2x1 or 3x1.

1x1 rib is typically used at the top of the sock

What you can do also is start with a 1x1 rib for say 30 rows and then swap out your ribber needles for cylinder needles to then produce a 2x1 rib for the leg of the sock.

KNITTING HEELS WITH THE RIBBER IN PLACE

If you want to have ribbing down the top of the foot of your sock you will need to swap out your ribber needles on the bottom of the foot to be all cylinder needles. To do this you will swap out all of the ribber needles in the front of the machine from hash mark to hash mark. And will knit the heel with the ribber in place (Gearhart machine you will need to swap out all ribber needles for cylinder needles and remove the ribber)

1. Swap ribber needles with cylinder needles in the front of the machine in-between hash marks
2. Remove ribber Drive Pin
3. Knit your heel
4. Place ribber Drive Pin back in after your heel is completed
5. Knit the foot
6. At this point you can swap out the rest of the ribber needles for cylinder needles and knit the toe.

Notes:

SELVAGE OR TOP HEM

To create a hem on the top of your sock there are many different ways, I will only cover 2 ways and I encourage you to look for a way that you like for your sock tops.

Hem Top

1. Start with scrap yarn, and all of your cylinder needles in the machine and crank about 4 inches with your scrap yarn
2. Tie on your sock yarn   (follow the directions from book one on making a hem top sock)
3. Crank maybe say 6 rounds
4. Hang the hem
5. Knit one round
6. Stop and now place your ribber on the machine
7. Swap out your cylinder needles to ribber needles for either a 2x1 or 3x1 rib
8. Knit the leg of your sock

Selvage with a 1x1 Rib

1. Start with scrap yarn and all your needles in the cylinder crank about 4 inches
2. Place your ribber on the machine
3. Swap out your cylinder needles so you have a 1x1 rib (1 cylinder needle and 1 ribber needle all the way around the machine)
4. Crank a couple rounds with your scrap yarn to ensure everything is working correctly
5. Cut your scrap yarn and tie on sock yarn
6. Crank around 1 time
7. Move the Selvage dial on your ribber to Out
8. Crank 2 rounds with the ribber in Out
9. Move the Selvage dial to In
10. Crank the leg of your sock

Selvage with a 2x1 Rib

1. Start with scrap yarn and all your needles in the cylinder crank about 4 inches
2. Place your ribber on the machine
3. Swap out your cylinder needles so you have a 2x1 rib (2 cylinder needles and 1 ribber needle all the way around the machine)
4. Crank a couple rounds with scrap yarn to ensure everything is working correctly
5. Cut your scrap yarn and tie on sock yarn
6. Crank around 1 time
7. Raise up the first cylinder needle to take it out of work, do this all the way around the machine raising the first of the pair of cylinder needles.
8. Crank around 1 or two times with the cylinder needles in this position
9. As you crank around the third time lower down each of the cylinder needles
10. Crank the leg of your sock

Notes:

ITEMS TO CHECK IF YOU ARE HAVING TROUBLE

These items below are some quick things you can check prior to making any adjustments on the machine.

Since I cannot be there with you right now as you are going though these things to check, what I will tell you are.

- Make any adjustment to your machine one thing at a time.
- Try one thing from this list and crank around and see if your ribber starts working better.
- Do one thing only if it helps GREAT . . . STOP and don't make any more adjustments.
- Only make another adjustment if the first one did not help.

How much weight are you using? Make sure you have all the black weights on the stem weight

Make sure your weight is being pulled down evenly you want the blue clothes pin or buckle to be even and the weight pulling down with the same pressure on the back of the machine as the front (the machines are very touchy about this.)

On the top of the ribber tappet plate is a switch that says In Out, or Rib Selvage   makes sure it is all the way to the IN or Rib position. Sometimes this switch will move just a hair and will need to be moved back to in or Rib.

Make sure the ribber arm is seated as far down in the holes on the cam shell as it will go there is an adjusting screw that should be touching the black part on the cam shell

Check to ensure the ribber drive pin is seated down fully in the hole on top of the ribber tappet   is should be in that hole   it looks like it is from the photos

Check your ribber & cylinder needles   make sure the little latches are not bent, and are moving freely (open/close)

ADJUSTMENTS TO THE MACHINE

The items below are all adjustments that can be made to your machine. It is very important to note again that if you make any adjustment to your machine, make small changes, and after you make one change crank around and see if that adjustment helped or made your situation worse. If it made it worse change it back. But if it helped and complete stitches are being formed stop and do not make any more adjustments.

Depending on the yarn, brand of yarn, thickness, weight, even sometimes color of yarn can make a small difference and some of these adjustments will need to be made   much like with a sewing machine   and sewing thick fabric vs. thin.   These are normal adjustments and are needed for the proper working of the sock machine.   This is why you always start with scrap yarn to ensure all needed adjustments are made prior to starting a real sock. Also ensure your scrap yarn is of the same weight, etc as your sock yarn you will be using. If in doubt knit the full skein of sock yarn you are going to use first into a tube make all your needed adjustments, then rewind that into a center pull ball or on a cone and then knit your sock.

Take all your ribber needles out and work with only one   maybe one at   about the 7 or the 4 o'clock position on the cylinder this way you can see on a angle what that one needle is doing

YARN CARRIER

Auto Knitter

On your yarn carrier there is a screw on the top this is the adjustment for the distance the yarn carrier is from the needles

Use a flat head screw driver and loosen the screw,

Move the yarn carrier head a hair closer to the needles   it should be fairly close   you do not want it so close that it is rubbing on the needles

Tighten the screw

Crank around slowly and see if that is any better   if it is worse move the carrier back

Legare

Sometimes what will happen on Legare machines is the yarn carrier might be a little bit too low and this will cause the ribber needle latches to catch on the yarn carrier. Loosen the screw on the base of the yarn carrier and raise it up just a hair, tighten the screw.

 Crank around and see if the latches now are not catching.

|  | Gearhart |

|  | Legare |

RIBBER TENSION

On the top of the ribber tappet plate you will see a large thumb screw and a pointer   on the tappet plate are little dashes

Loosen this screw and move the pointer so it is pointing at the center dash

Tighten the screw and crank around a couple times and see if the stitches form better

This is how you adjust the size of the ribber (purl) stitches,   depending on the yarn you may need to loosen or tighten this to get the fabric you like.

	Gearhart Tension
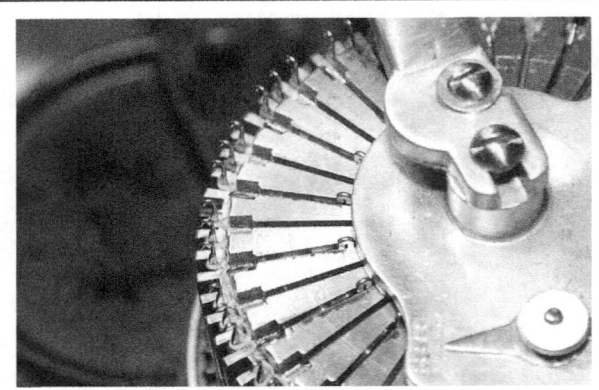	

RIBBER HEIGHT

Adjust is the ribber height if the above item did not correct it

You will need a flat head screw driver

On the ribber arm you will see a screw, screw this in maybe half a turn (the machines need very little adjustments, a small amount when adjusting is better)

After you adjust the screw push down a bit on the ribber arm just to make sure it is all the way down

When lowering the screw what you should see is the ribber going down lower bringing it closer to the top of the cylinder make sure all the ribber needles are empty, no stitches on them and you may want to only have one ribber needle in the machine for this, crank around once it will make that half stitch crank around again does it make a complete stitch? If not lower it down a little more

Gearhart Ribber Height

Harmony / Auto Knitter

Legare

RIBBER TIMING

To adjust the timing this may have gotten bumped or loosened during shipping

You will need a flat head screw driver

On the ribber tappet plate where the ribber drive pin goes into that hole   on the silver part looks kinda like a kidney bean shape (good technical description right) there is a screw on the one end. This is the timing adjustment.

Loosen that screw, move it slightly very slight (it does not take a lot) forward,   tighten the screw

You may want to take out all but one of the ribber needles for this step   just pull them out and don't worry about them stitches running   no need to put the cylinder needles back in either just pull the ribber needles out

Now crank   very slowly around and watch that one ribber needle,   watch to see if the yarn coming from the carrier is being caught by the ribber needle, if the yarn is not,   you will need to set the timing back the other way just a hair.

This timing adjustment determines when the needles come out, go back in, and make stitches. If it is set to soon the yarn coming out of the carrier will miss the needle, and if it is set to late it will also miss the needle you have to get it set at just the right spot so the yarn coming from the yarn carrier lays right there ready for the ribber needle to grab it when the needle starts to pull back in.

The ribber is not a hard item to use; once you get it adjusted and set you should not have to adjust it again. The thing that makes the ribber different to use is the fact that you can no longer see down into the cylinder as you are knitting. As always practice with tubes till you can knit with the ribber on and not have holes, dropped stitches etc.

I hope this book can help you learn how the ribber works.

Donna Peters

Made in the USA
Las Vegas, NV
04 July 2024

91861092R00024